Scarlet and the Ring

Meg and Greg

Scarlet and the Ring

with **ar or er air**

Four Phonics Stories

Written by
Elspeth Rae and Rowena Rae

Illustrated by
Elisa Gutiérrez

ORCA BOOK PUBLISHERS

Published in Canada and the United States in 2023 by Orca Book Publishers.
orcabook.com

Library and Archives Canada Cataloguing in Publication
Title: Scarlet and the ring : with four phonics stories /
written by Elspeth Rae and Rowena Rae ; illustrated by Elisa Gutiérrez.
Names: Rae, Elspeth, 1973- author. | Rae, Rowena, author. | Gutiérrez, Elisa, 1972- illustrator.
Series: Rae, Elspeth, 1973- Meg and Greg ; bk. 4. | Orca two read.
Description: Series statement: Meg and Greg ; book 4 |
Orca two read | Practices the sounds ar, or, er, and air.
Identifiers: Canadiana (print) 20220174407 | Canadiana (ebook) 20220174415 |
ISBN 9781459824997 (softcover) | ISBN 9781459825000 (PDF) | ISBN 9781459825017 (EPUB)
Subjects: LCSH: Reading—Phonetic method—Problems, exercises, etc. |
LCSH: Reading—Phonetic method—Study and teaching (Elementary)
Classification: LCC PS8635.A39 S32 2023 | DDC jC813/.6—dc23

Library of Congress Control Number: 2022933273

Summary: This partially illustrated workbook, meant to be read by an advanced reader with a beginner reader or struggling reader, combines stories and exercises that focus on phonics and fostering literacy.

Orca Book Publishers is committed to reducing the consumption of nonrenewable resources in the production of our books. We make every effort to use materials that support a sustainable future.

Orca Book Publishers gratefully acknowledges the support for its publishing programs provided by the following agencies: the Government of Canada, the Canada Council for the Arts and the Province of British Columbia through the BC Arts Council and the Book Publishing Tax Credit.

Design and illustration by Elisa Gutiérrez

Printed and bound in Canada.

26 25 24 23 • 1 2 3 4

In this book:

ar

or

er

air

Contents

How to read the stories in this book

Adult or buddy reader's text

Kid's text

Chapter 1

Stardust Market

Meg stood at the railing of the ferryboat as it approached **Stardust** Island. "We're almost there, Greg!"

Greg didn't look up. "Let me finish this chapter. Detective **Smart** is solving the case!"

Meg grinned. "Did your cousin **Martha** get a dog?"

Greg looked up. "What? Oh yes, a new puppy named **Scarlet**."

"I see them. But not your aunt **Carmen**," Meg said.

"My aunt is probably at the **farmers' market**. She has a jewelry stall," Greg said.

Meg smiled. "I love **farmers' markets!**"

Greg rubbed his tummy. "Me too! I love all the yummy treats for sale."

On the dock, **Martha** gave Greg a big hug.

Hi Meg! This is **Scarlet**.

Hi **Martha**.

I am so glad you came with Greg to visit us!

Let's go to the **market** and get lunch.

Meg and Greg is a series of decodable phonics storybooks for children ages 6 to 9 who are struggling to learn how to read because of **dyslexia** or another language-based learning difficulty. The stories are designed for a child and an experienced reader to share the reading, as shown in the diagram above. A child feeling overwhelmed at reading sentences could start by reading only the illustration labels. More about this approach is on page 152.

What is included in these stories

The stories in this book are for a child who is familiar with all the basic **consonant** sounds (including **consonant blends**), **short vowel sounds** and the thirteen **phonograms** and spellings introduced in *Meg and Greg* Book 1 (*ck, sh, ch, th*), Book 2 (*nk, ng, tch, dge*) and Book 3 (*a-e, e-e, i-e, o-e, u-e*).

The stories in this book focus on words pronounced with vowel sounds controlled by the letter *r*. They are known as *r***-controlled** or bossy *r* words. We introduce the sounds—shown inside slashes—in this order: **/ar/** (*star*), **/or/** (*north, door, more*), **/er/** (*her, bird, turn*) and **/air/** (*fair, bear, parent, carrot, heron, errand*). Some of these spellings are pronounced differently in some accents.

The stories also use a few common words that can be tricky to sound out, listed to the right. Find out more on pages 148–149.

A note about /or/, /er/ and /air/
For the first time, we have written stories that introduce multiple spellings for a single sound. More on page 150.

Suffixes
Also look out for a few suffixes (*-ing* and *-er*) in some of these stories. More on page 151.

Warning!

These words look little, but they can be tricky to read.

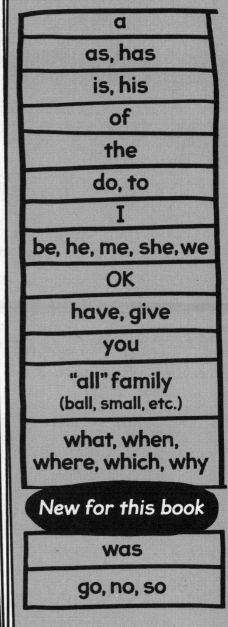

a

as, has

is, his

of

the

do, to

I

be, he, me, she, we

OK

have, give

you

"all" family
(ball, small, etc.)

what, when, where, which, why

New for this book

was

go, no, so

All the stories in
this book introduce words
that contain an *r-controlled vowel*.
When the letter *r* appears with a vowel,
the pronunciation of the vowel is very
different from its short or long sound.
Consider the difference between the
pronunciation of the vowel in *băn* (**short
vowel**) and *barn* (*r*-controlled vowel).

This story focuses on words containing
the sound **/ar/** as in *sharp* and *star*.
This sound is only spelled with the *ar*
phonogram, which can appear anywhere
in a syllable: at the beginning, as in *art*; in
the middle, as in *farm*; or at the end, as in
mar-ket. (We do not include the suffix *-ar*,
as in *lunar*, which is pronounced differently.)

The story also includes the thirteen
phonograms and spellings introduced in
Meg and Greg Book 1 (*ck, sh, ch, th*), Book 2
(*nk, ng, tch, dge*) and Book 3 (*a-e, e-e, i-e,
o-e, u-e*).

For a list of words with the sound **/ar/**,
including all the ones used in this
story, go to orcatworead.com.

Scarlet
and the
Ring

A story featuring the sound

market

Plum Tarts

Carmen

Chard

Scarlet

Martha

Stardust Market

Meg stood at the railing of the ferryboat as it approached **Stardust** Island.

"We're almost there, Greg. Stop reading your book!"

Greg didn't look up. "Let me finish this chapter. Detective **Smart** is solving the case!"

Meg grinned. "Did your cousin **Martha** get a dog?"

Greg looked up. "What? Oh yes, a new puppy named **Scarlet**."

"I see them. But not your aunt **Carmen**," Meg said.

"My aunt is probably at the **farmers' market**. She has a jewelry stall," Greg said.

Meg smiled. "I love **farmers' markets**!"

Greg rubbed his tummy. "Me too! I love all the yummy treats for sale."

Martha led the way along a path, following the signs to **Stardust Farm Market**.

Greg held **Scarlet's** leash. He looked up at his cousin. "**Are** you finished college for the summer?"

Martha nodded. "Yup, I had my last exam on Tuesday. It's nice to be home for a few months. I'm excited to hang out with you two."

"I've told Meg about all the amazing stuff we can do here," Greg said.

Meg nodded. "Greg said you have a friend with horses."

"Yes, I do! My friend Flora has two horses," **Martha** replied.

ar

At the **market**, vendors were setting up stalls. The three kids walked through, looking at all the things for sale.

Greg saw a sign that read *Grub* ***Garden***. "Does 'grub' mean food? I'm **starving**!"

Martha laughed. "Yes, it does."

Meg groaned. "You **are** *always* hungry."

"Let's find my mom. We can drop off your bags at her jewelry stall," **Martha** said. "Then we can get some lunch."

Chapter 2

The Lost **Garnet** Ring

Aunt **Carmen** went back to hunting through a box on her table.

"When did you last see the ring?" Meg asked.

Carmen looked up. "Goodness! How rude of me. You must be Meg. I'm so pleased to meet you." She came out from behind her stall. "Please forgive me. I'm just so worried about the missing **garnet** ring."

Meg smiled. "It's OK. We can help you find it."

Scarlet

"What if somebody stole it?" **Martha** asked.

Carmen frowned. "I hope not. The **market** has only just opened for the day."

"Did you see anyone looking at your jewelry?" Meg asked.

"No, nobody," **Carmen** said. "It's just been me and a few birds, until you three got here."

"Birds? What kind of birds?" Greg asked.

"A few different ones. Robins, chickadees, **starlings** . . . " **Carmen** said.

Greg frowned. "I've read that **starlings** sometimes take bits of string and wool to make their nests. But not jewelry."

Chapter 3

Scarlet on the Case

Meg **started** looking up at the trees. "Don't worry, **Carmen**. Greg and I will find the **starling's** nest and get your ring back."

Carmen sighed. "Thank you, Meg."

"This is exciting," Greg said. "Just like Detective **Smart** in my book, we **are** on a case—the Case of the **Garnet** Ring!"

"I'll stay here and help my mom," **Martha** said. "Good luck. I hope you two find it!"

Greg nodded and turned to Meg. "There **are** lots of trees behind the kids' **park**."

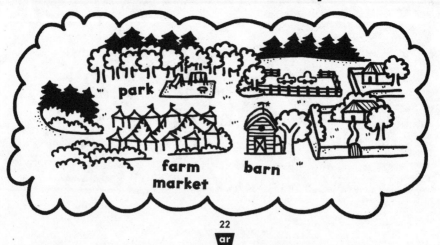

park

farm
market

barn

Greg looked up to see what **Scarlet** was **barking** at. "A nest! **Scarlet**, you **smart** dog!"

"That branch is too **hard** to reach," Meg said. "We **are** going to need a ladder."

Greg nodded. "Where will we find a ladder?"

"I saw one behind the **barn** on the **far** side of the **market**," Meg said. "Let's ask someone if we could borrow it."

barn

Meg and Greg took the ladder back to the **park**. They leaned it against the tree with the nest. **Scarlet started barking** again.

"**Scarlet**!" Greg said. "What **are** you **barking** at now?"

The dog **darted** across the **park**.

kids' park

"**Scarlet**, come back!" Greg cried.

Meg **started** down the ladder. "Greg! She's chasing something. It looks like a chipmunk."

"Ugh." Greg groaned. "Just what we need. We're detectives on a case, and **Scarlet** goes off on a chase."

Meg shook her head. "I can see something hanging from the chipmunk's mouth."

Greg's eyes lit up. "Is it the ring?

Chapter 4

On Top of the **Barn**

Meg jumped off the ladder and ran after Greg. "Can you see **Scarlet**?"

"She's under those trees," Greg called back.

Meg caught up with Greg. "Where? I can't see her."

"She just went behind that line of **parked cars**," Greg said.

"You go that way, Greg. I'll go this way," Meg said.

Meg and Greg ran to **Scarlet**. She had her front legs up on one side of the **barn**, and she was **barking** wildly.

Meg looked up. "The chipmunk is on the roof! It's sitting on top of the weather vane!"

"Can you still see the pink **yarn** in its mouth?" Greg asked.

Meg nodded. "Yes, and something shiny is hanging from the **yarn**. That must be the **garnet** ring!"

kids' park

star

Greg scanned the ground and spotted an old net on a long pole. "Let's use this to catch the chipmunk."

"OK, but we need to be up higher." Meg walked to the other side of the **barn**. "Greg! There's a stack of hay bales."

"Perfect," Greg said. He climbed up the hay. "Keep your eye on the little guy."

The chipmunk sat on the weather vane, flicking its tail. Suddenly it hopped down to the **barn** roof and **darted** away.

"Greg! It's on the roof," Meg said.

"**Darn**," Greg said.

"It jumped," Meg shouted. "It's on that string of flags!"

barn

stump

garden wall

Chapter 5

Bart's Garden

Meg peered over the wall. "I can see the chipmunk! And I can see the **garnet** ring hanging from the **yarn**."

"Great!" Greg climbed up next to Meg. "But we still have to catch the thief."

"Oh!" Meg cried. "It went into a hole at the base of that big tree!"

"Let's hope it stays there," Greg said.

"Look!" Meg said. "It **darted** back out, but it doesn't have the **yarn** or the ring!"

Greg grinned. "Perfect."

garden wall

stump

Greg drummed his fingers on the gate. "I bet Aunt **Carmen** knows who lives here. Let's go ask her."

Meg nodded. "And we should ask permission to go into someone's **garden** anyway. You go, and I'll keep an eye on the chipmunk!"

Greg and **Scarlet** ran back to the **market**.

"Great news!" Greg shouted as he got close to **Carmen's** stall. "We found your ring. A chipmunk stole it and hid it in its hole!"

Carmen clapped. "Thank you!"

"But we don't have it yet," Greg said. "The chipmunk's hole is in that **garden** with the stone wall."

Martha led the way to **Bart's** stall. Greg and **Scarlet** trotted close behind.

"Hello, **are** you **Bart**?" **Martha** asked the man standing at **Bart's** Cakes and **Tarts**.

"Yes!" the man replied. "**Are** you **Carmen's** daughter?"

Martha nodded. "I am, and this is my cousin Greg. We came to ask for your help."

"A chipmunk stole one of Aunt **Carmen's** rings," Greg said, "and hid it in a hole at the base of the huge tree in your **garden**!"

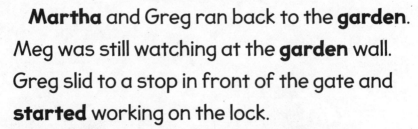

Martha and Greg ran back to the **garden**. Meg was still watching at the **garden** wall. Greg slid to a stop in front of the gate and **started** working on the lock.

"Is the chipmunk in its hole?" **Martha** asked.

"Not right now," Meg said. "It keeps **darting** in and out. But I think the **garnet** ring is still in there."

Inside the **garden**, the three kids knelt beside the hole.

"Now what?" Greg asked.

"Stick your **arm** into the hole," Meg said. Greg frowned.

sharp

The End

Turn the page for more practice with the /ar/ sound!

ar
spelling

Spell each *ar* word below the picture.
One letter fits into each box.

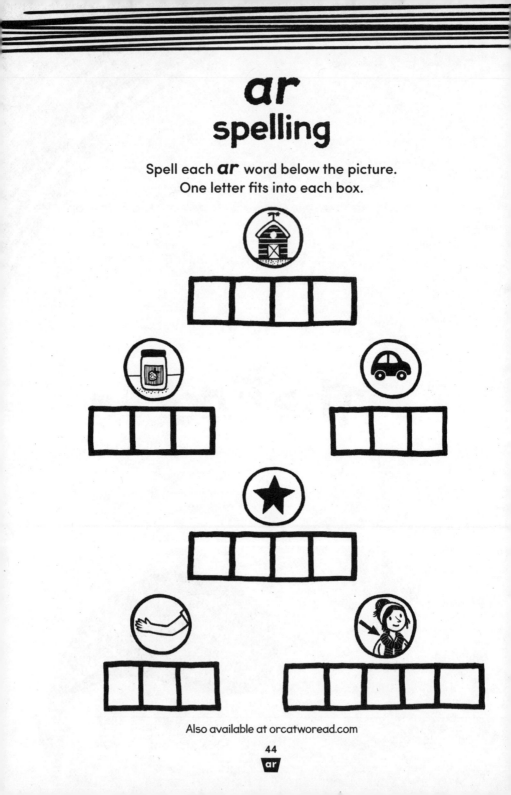

ar
word ladder

Climb down the ladder by solving the clues and changing just one sound from the previous **ar** word. You'll know you've done it right if the word at the bottom of the ladder matches the one at the top.

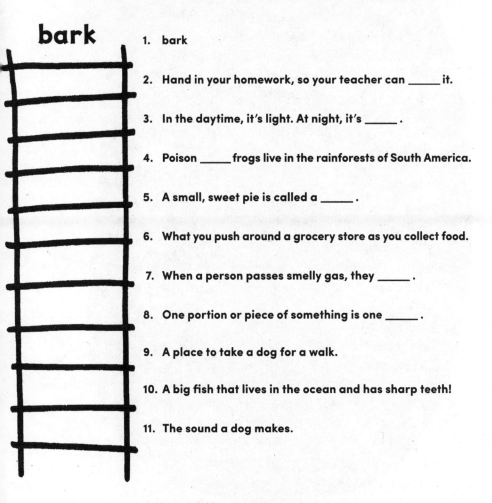

bark

1. bark

2. Hand in your homework, so your teacher can _____ it.

3. In the daytime, it's light. At night, it's _____ .

4. Poison _____ frogs live in the rainforests of South America.

5. A small, sweet pie is called a _____ .

6. What you push around a grocery store as you collect food.

7. When a person passes smelly gas, they _____ .

8. One portion or piece of something is one _____ .

9. A place to take a dog for a walk.

10. A big fish that lives in the ocean and has sharp teeth!

11. The sound a dog makes.

Also available at orcatworead.com

All the stories in this book introduce words that contain an **r-controlled vowel**. When the letter *r* appears with a vowel, the pronunciation of the vowel is very different from its short or long sound. Consider the difference between the pronunciation of the vowel in *pŏt* (**short vowel**) and *port* (r-controlled vowel).

This story focuses on words containing the sound **/or/**, which is most frequently spelled with the **phonogram** *or* (*corn*). We have also included the phonograms *oor* (*door*) and *ore* (*more*), because they appear in some common words.

Other ways to spell the sound **/or/** include *oar* (*board*), *our* (*four*) and *ar* when following a *w* (*war, warn*). These phonograms are not included in this story. We also do not include the suffix -*or*, as in *doctor*, which is pronounced differently.

The *or* phonogram can appear anywhere in a syllable: at the beginning, as in *orbit*; in the middle, as in *storm*; or at the end, as in *for*. The *oor* and *ore* phonograms only appear at the end of a syllable (*poor, store*).

This story also includes **/ar/** words for continued practice, as well as the thirteen phonograms and spellings introduced in *Meg and Greg* Book 1 (*ck, sh, ch, th*), Book 2 (*nk, ng, tch, dge*) and Book 3 (*a-e, e-e, i-e, o-e, u-e*).

For a list of words with the sound **/or/**, including all the ones used in this story, go to orcatworead.com.

A Lost Horse

A story featuring the sound

forest

or

North Fort

camping

horse prints

Flora

Chapter 1

Camping at **North** Cove

Meg hammered the last tent peg into the sand.

"Wow, you got the tent up quickly!" Martha said.

Greg grinned. "We had lots of practice when we went to Camp Nut-Hatch."

He was setting up a campstove while Martha stabbed a **fork** into a packet of hot dogs.

"This is an awesome campsite!" Meg said.

Martha nodded. "This beach at **North** Cove is the best camping spot on Stardust Island. I come here a lot with my friends **Flora** and Amber."

• •

"**Popcorn!**"

Greg looked up. "Did you guys hear that?"

"**Popcorn**!"

Martha stared into the **forest**. "That's definitely **Flora's** voice."

"I see someone coming out of the trees," Greg said, pointing down the beach. "Is that her?"

Martha waved. "**Flora**! Is everything OK?"

"Hi Martha!" **Flora** said. "**Popcorn** got spooked and threw me off."

"Are you hurt?" Martha asked.

"I'm OK, but I can't find **Popcorn**," **Flora** said.

"We'll help you," Martha said.

"Thanks!" **Flora** smiled.

"This is my cousin Greg and his friend Meg," Martha added.

Greg nodded. "And Meg knows a lot about **horses**. She goes every summer to her aunt and uncle's ranch."

Chapter 2

On the Hunt
for Popcorn

Flora, Martha, Meg and Greg headed **for** the **forest**.

"If Detective Smart were here, he would look **for** clues on the **forest floor**," Greg said.

Meg grinned. "You are so into those Detective Smart books, Greg."

Flora nodded. "You're right, Greg. Maybe we can find his hoofprints. Then we can track him."

"**Popcorn!**" Martha called.

Popcorn!

For the next hour, **Flora**, Martha, Meg and Greg searched the **forest**.

Greg kicked a pile of **acorns**. "I was sure we would find **more** clues."

"What about checking by the stream?" Martha asked.

Flora nodded. "Good idea. If **Popcorn** went **for** a drink, we might find his hoofprints."

They found the stream and followed it **for** as far as they could.

"No sign of a **horse**," Meg said.

"**Popcorn**! Where are you?" **Flora** called.

Flora

Flora pulled up her hood. "**Popcorn** should be OK if he can find shelter **for** the night."

"We can look **for more** clues in the **morning**," Greg said.

Flora nodded. "Yes, but now I have another problem. I was planning to camp out, but my tent and sleeping bag are in **Popcorn's** saddlebags."

"No problem!" Martha said. "We have room **for** you. Our tent is huge, and we have lots of food."

Flora smiled. "Thank you, Martha. It's so lucky that I ran into you!"

camp site

Chapter 3

Hornets!

fog

Honk-onk!

"That **foghorn** sounds so spooky," Meg said.

Flora gazed into the fog. "I was lying awake listening to the **foghorn** this **morning**. I was wondering where to look **for Popcorn**."

"There's the stream in the **forest**," Martha said. "He might try to get a drink this **morning**."

Flora nodded. "**Or** he could have gone to the fruit trees near the old **fort**. He likes to eat fallen fruit."

Greg blew on his hot chocolate. "Should we split up and check both places?"

Meg and **Flora** set off along the beach to the old **fort**.

"Why were fruit trees planted next to the **fort**?" Meg asked.

Flora shrugged. "I guess to feed the people who used to live at the **fort**."

"I bet you're right about **Popcorn** going to eat fruit," Meg said. "The **horses** on my aunt's ranch love apples."

Flora smiled and looked up. "Here we are. That's the **fort** up there."

Martha and Greg walked through the **forest**.

"With luck, we'll find **Popcorn** at the stream having a drink," Martha said.

"**Or** if he's not there," Greg said, "he might have left **horse** footprints in the mud."

Martha smiled. "**Flora** calls them hoofprints."

"**Popcorn**!" Martha called as they got close to the stream.

Greg clapped his hands. "Look! **Horse** footprints in the mud!"

"*Hoofprints*. He was here!" Martha said.

horse prints

Chapter 4

Snort! Snort!

Meg, Greg and Martha ran out of the **forest** and toward the old **fort**.

"Oh! **Poor** you," Martha said when they got to **Flora**. "**Hornets** stung you on *both* feet?"

Flora made a face as she nodded.

"Let's get your feet in the cold seawater," Meg said. "That might take away the pain."

"That feels better," **Flora** said. "Back to **Popcorn**. I think I saw him!"

"Meg says she has spent a lot of time with the **horses** on her aunt's ranch," **Flora** said.

Martha raised her eyebrows. "I know, but **Popcorn** is *such* a big **horse**."

Meg smiled. "No bigger than my uncle's **horse**, Black Jack. I ride him at the ranch all the time."

Greg's eyes sparkled. "I know about **horses** too! I went with Meg to the ranch last summer. And we even saved the **horses** and all the other animals from a wildfire!"

"It sounds like you two will be just fine," **Flora** said.

Chapter 5

Plums **for Popcorn**

horse

Popcorn ran a **short** distance away. Then he turned and looked at Meg and Greg.

"**Popcorn**," Meg said softly. "We're here to take you back to **Flora**." She turned to Greg. "You go that way, and I'll go this way . . . "

"**Snort!**"

"He keeps backing away," Meg said. "We need a treat **or** something **for** him."

Greg picked a handful of grass. "How about this?"

"We almost had him," Meg said.

Greg looked around. "I'll get some fruit from the plum trees. Maybe he'll like that."

Meg nodded. "Good idea, Greg. Just watch out **for hornets**!"

Greg came back with his hands filled with fruit. "Look, **Popcorn**. A plum. Yum, yum!"

Meg laughed. The **horse snorted** softly and took a few steps toward Greg.

"Good boy," Meg said. "Were you OK in the big **storm** last night?"

Greg wrinkled his nose. "Ooh! That tickles!"

Popcorn

plums

Meg held **Popcorn's** reins, and Greg rubbed his neck.

They walked him past the old **fort** and down the hill. As they got close to the beach, Martha spotted them and waved. "Yippee!"

Popcorn trotted down the beach to **Flora** and laid his head on her shoulder. "**Snort!**"

Flora reached up to hug **Popcorn**.

forest

North Fort

The End

Turn the page for more practice with the /or/ sound!

or
spelling

Spell each **or** word below the picture.
One letter fits into each box.

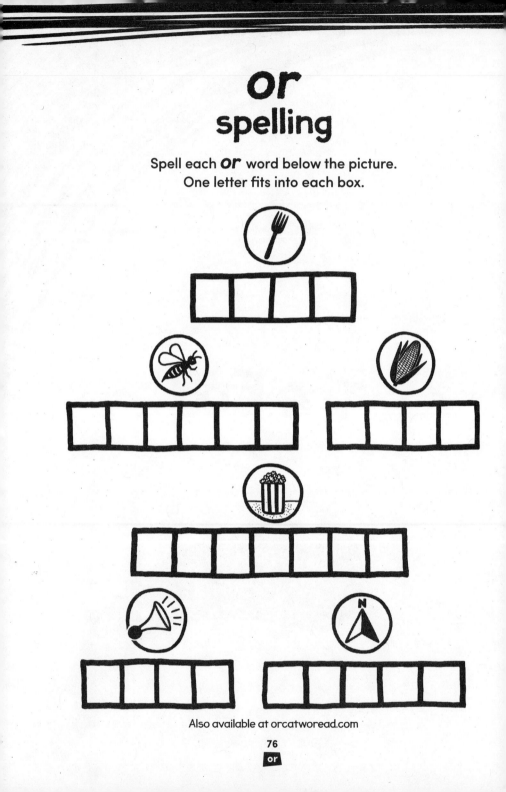

or

crossword

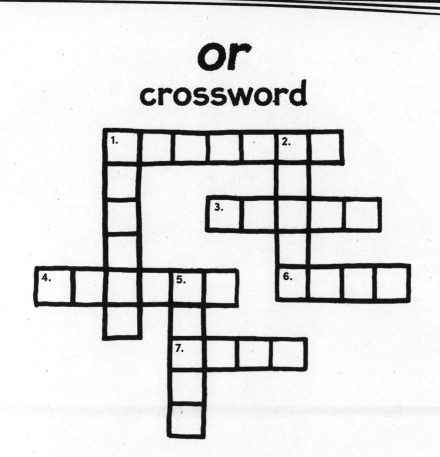

Across ➡

1. A person who sells flowers.
3. When there is lots of rain, wind, thunder and lightning, we call it a _____.
4. Baseball, soccer, hockey and tennis are all _____.
6. Another word for *ripped* is _____.
7. A whale with black and white markings; also called a killer whale.

Down ⬇

1. The past tense of forget.
2. The opposite of tall.
5. The sharp, pointy spike on the stem of a rose is called a _____.

Also available at orcatworead.com

All the stories in
this book introduce words that
contain an **r-controlled vowel**. When the
letter *r* appears with a vowel, the pronunciation
of the vowel is very different from its short or long
sound. Consider the difference between the
pronunciation of the vowel in *bĭd* (**short vowel**)
and *bird* (r-controlled vowel).

This story focuses on words containing the
sound **/er/** spelled with the three most common
phonograms for this sound, which are *er* (*her*), *ir*
(*bird*) and *ur* (*turn*). Other ways to spell the sound
/er/ include the two suffixes -*or* as in *actor* and -*ar* as
in *dollar* and also the phonograms *ar* (*orchard*), *ear*
(*earth*), *our* (*journal*) and *yr* (*syrup*). These less common
phonograms have not been included in this story.

The *er, ir* and *ur* phonograms can appear anywhere
in a syllable but are most commonly in the middle (*fern,
girl, surf*).

This story also includes **/ar/** and **/or/** words
for continued practice, as well as the thirteen
phonograms and spellings introduced in *Meg and
Greg* Book 1 (*ck, sh, ch, th*), Book 2 (*nk, ng, tch,
dge*) and Book 3 (*a-e, e-e, i-e, o-e, u-e*).
For a list of words with the sound **/er/**,
including all the ones used in this story,
go to orcatworead.com.

Surf Lessons

A story featuring the sound

bird

camera

tether strap

Amber

surf

Chapter 1

To the **Surf**

Greg's aunt Carmen stopped **her** car in the **Pender** Cove parking lot. **Everyone** piled out. Greg held Scarlet on **her** leash. Meg held **her** new **camera**. Greg's cousin Martha and **her** friend **Amber** pulled four **surfboards** off the roof of the car.

Carmen waved. "Have fun, kids! Use that sunblock I gave you. I don't want to see any **sunburns** at **dinner** this evening."

Martha waved back. "We'll be careful, Mom!"

Amber

The four kids followed the trail to the beach.

"I'm so excited to try **surfing**!" Meg said.

Martha smiled. "It's a lot of fun once you get the hang of it."

Amber nodded. "It can be a bit hard at **first**, but we'll help you."

"Martha tried to teach me last **summer**," Greg said. "I **never** even stood up on the board!"

"It was too stormy that week," Martha said. "It's hard to get started in big waves."

tether strap

Martha showed Meg how to wrap the **tether** strap around **her** ankle. "This way you won't lose your board when you fall off," Martha explained.

They all waded into the **water** with their boards.

"**First** let's practice standing up on the board and balancing," Martha said.

Greg frowned as he knelt and then carefully rose on his feet. "I did it!" He waved. "Look at me. Ack!" *Splash!*

"Almost, Greg," **Amber** said. "Try again!"

"Bark! Bark!"

Meg looked **over**. "What's Scarlet up to? She's way down the beach."

Chapter 2

A Lost **Surfer**?

Martha splashed into the **water** and grabbed the upside-down **surfboard**.

Amber scratched **her** head. "A broken **surfboard** with no **surfer**. That's not a good sign."

Martha frowned. "Did someone leave their board too close to the **water** and a wave swept it away?"

"**Perhaps**, but I can't imagine a **surfer** being so careless," **Amber** said. She scanned the **water**.

"Is the **tether** strap still attached, Martha?" Meg asked.

Martha reached into the **water**. "Only part of it. The Velcro bit that wraps around the ankle has ripped off."

"I think we should get up to **higher** ground for a **better** look at the **water**," **Amber** said.

Greg **turned** and scanned the beach. "**Over** there. We can climb up those big rocks."

They all ran to the rocks.

rocks

surf

"We need to look **farther** out," **Amber** said, pointing. "Lots of people **surf** the waves **over** by that headland."

Greg frowned. "It looks rough out there."

Greg and Martha jumped down to the sand and followed Scarlet. **Amber** and Meg stayed on the rocks and scanned the **water.**

"What did you find, Scarlet?" Greg asked as they got **closer.**

"A bag, a **T-shirt** and a towel," Martha said.

Greg frowned. "Only one **person's** things. So somebody must have come **surfing** alone."

Martha nodded. "Maybe **Amber** will know whose stuff this is."

Chapter 3

Scarlet the **Swimmer**

Amber squinted again at the **water.** "Maybe **Kirk** lost his board out there and swam to shore, but with the **current** he ended up in the next cove **over.**"

"Should we try getting around to the next cove then?" asked Meg.

Amber frowned. "Yes, but I don't know if there's a path."

Martha nodded. "I'll go back and grab a couple of our boards, in case we need them to paddle around."

Greg tried to whistle like Martha did **whenever** she called Scarlet. "Come, Scarlet!"

Scarlet kept on swimming.

Meg shielded **her** eyes from the sun. "It looks like she's swimming to that little rocky island."

Greg tried whistling again. "Scarlet! That's too far! Come back!"

rocks

Scarlet

surf

As Martha got **closer** with the boards, **Amber turned** back toward the rocky headland. "I'll keep looking for a path."

"I'll come with you," Meg said.

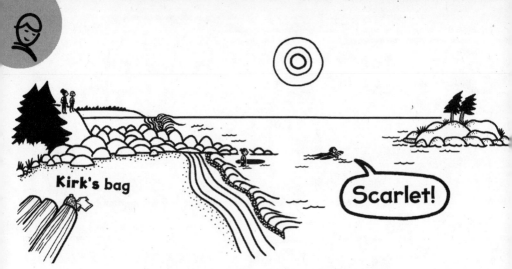

Kirk's bag

Scarlet!

Amber and Meg were now high above the beach, looking for a way down to the next cove. Martha's voice carried on the breeze. "Scarlet!"

Amber laughed. "Martha **sure** has **her** hands full with that puppy!"

Meg **turned** toward the **water**. "Look! Scarlet is all the way out on that little island."

Amber shook **her** head. "I can't believe she swam that far!"

Meg scrunched up **her** eyes. "**Amber**, can I have my **camera** from your bag?"

Chapter 4

A **Monster** Wave

Amber and Meg leaped down the rocks and sprinted toward Greg. Martha was close to the rocky island.

"We think **Kirk** is on the far side of that little island," Meg shouted as they got **closer**.

"And Scarlet has a hat in **her** mouth. I bet it's **Kirk's**," **Amber** said.

Greg stood holding the spare **surfboard**. "Martha thought it was a dead **bird**!"

Amber shook **her** head and started wading into the **water**. "Wait for one of us, Martha."

rocks

Martha and Greg pulled their boards
ashore where Scarlet stood barking at them.

Martha ruffled the **fur** on Scarlet's head.
"Good **girl**!"

Scarlet bounded away across the rocks.
Martha and Greg scrambled **after her**.

"**Kirk**?" Greg asked.

A young **surfer** was leaning against a rock,
with one leg **curled** up. A Velcro strap was
around the ankle of his **other** leg.

Martha knelt next to him. "I'm Martha,
Amber's friend."

Kirk tried to sit up but winced. "Hi Martha.
I'm so happy to see you guys."

surfer

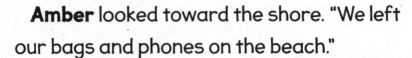

Amber looked toward the shore. "We left our bags and phones on the beach."

Martha stood up. "I'll go back and call for an ambulance."

Greg nodded. "And the three of us will get **Kirk** back to shore."

rocks

shore

Meg **turned** to Greg. "Let's bring our **surfboards** around. **Kirk** can sit on one, and we can tow him to the beach."

"I'll stay here," **Amber** said. She knelt and started examining **Kirk's hurt** leg. "They're Meg and Greg. Greg is Martha's cousin."

Chapter 5

A **Surf** Lesson

Greg scanned the small island. "We need something to hold his leg still."

Meg nodded. "I saw some sticks on the **other** side of the island. Maybe we can make a splint."

Amber looked up at Meg and Greg. "Good idea."

Scarlet followed them **over** the rocks.

"We can use the broken **tether** strap to attach the sticks to your leg," **Amber** said, reaching down to take it off **Kirk's** ankle.

tether strap

Meg stood with **her** hands on **her** hips. "That looks good. Now we need to get you onto a **surfboard**."

rocks

leg
splint

Kirk shifted sideways a tiny bit. "I think now I can shuffle **over** to the **water**. Can one of you lift my **hurt** leg?"

Amber nodded. Greg and Meg waded into the **water** to hold one of the **surfboards** still. **Kirk** took a deep breath.

By the time they reached the beach, Martha was leading an ambulance crew down from the parking lot.

One paramedic examined **Kirk**. "It's your knee. Quite a common **injury** for a **surfer**. You may also have bruised a few ribs, and you got yourself a pretty bad **sunburn**."

Kirk nodded. "A **monster** wave got me and slammed me onto the rocks."

"You're lucky your friends found you," the paramedic added.

kit

tether strap

The End

Turn the page for more practice with the /er/ sound!

ir
spelling

Spell each *ir* word below the picture.
One letter fits into each box.

er sound
word search

Find the words listed below in the puzzle.
Words are hidden ➜ and ↓.

```
b  n  l  y  t  a  p  h  a  c  a  s
u  u  z  t  h  j  s  e  n  e  y  w
r  r  b  e  i  n  e  r  v  e  f  i
s  s  u  r  r  m  p  m  x  r  i  r
t  e  r  m  s  r  r  i  t  x  r  l
p  n  n  w  t  e  w  t  q  g  m  v
c  u  r  l  r  a  f  e  r  n  f  x
p  p  s  q  u  i  r  m  v  x  u  t
```

burn	firm	squirm
burst	hermit	swirl
curl	nerve	term
fern	nurse	thirst

All the stories in this book introduce words that contain an **r-controlled vowel**. When the letter *r* appears with a vowel, the pronunciation of the vowel is very different from its short or long sound. Consider the difference between the pronunciation of the vowels in *hāil* (**long vowel**) and *hair* (*r*-controlled vowel).

This story focuses on words containing the sound /**air**/, which is often spelled with the **phonogram** *air* as in *fair*. The *air* phonogram appears most commonly at the end of a syllable (*chair*). We have also included five less frequent phonograms that make the sound /**air**/: *ear* (*bear*), *arr*+vowel (*parrot*), *ar*+vowel (*care*), *er*+vowel (*there*) and *err*+vowel (*Ferris*).

This story also includes /**ar**/, /**or**/ and /**er**/ words for continued practice, as well as the thirteen phonograms and spellings introduced in *Meg and Greg* Book 1 (*ck, sh, ch, th*), Book 2 (*nk, ng, tch, dge*) and Book 3 (*a-e, e-e, i-e, o-e, u-e*). For a list of words with the sound /**air**/, including all the ones used in this story, go to orcatworead.com.

The Bear in the Air

A story featuring the sound

Ferris Fun Ride

heron

air

fair

bear

Harris

Stardust Fun **Fair**

"Whee! This is fun, **Harris**!" Martha said to the little boy sitting next to her on the jungle ride.

"Hold on tight!" Meg and Greg called from the seat behind.

Martha, Meg and Greg were babysitting three-year-old **Harris** for the day. They were at the Stardust Fun **Fair**.

"Birdie," **Harris** said, pointing.

"Yes," Martha said. "A **parrot**. **Parrots** live in the jungle, and this is a jungle ride."

Greg leaned forward. "Which ride do you want to try next, **Harris**?"

"Let's go on the roller coaster!" Meg said.

116

"Wow, this is a long line," Meg said. "The **airplane** ride is popular."

Martha looked at **Harris**. "Are you sure you want to wait? The line is really long."

"Yes!" **Harris** cried. "**Blair** loves **airplanes**."

Meg **stared** at the crowd around them. "Oh, look! Those people are dressed up as vegetables!"

Greg turned. "What? That's funny!"

Martha laughed. "They do this every year to celebrate Stardust Island's farms."

The vegetable mascots were handing out balloons to kids.

"**Blair** likes balloons!" **Harris** wiggled in Martha's arms, and she set him on the ground. He ran to the **carrot** mascot.

Harris beamed. "One balloon for me and one for **Blair**!"

"What a lucky **bear**," Martha said. She led **Harris** back to the line for the **airplane** ride.

Greg counted the people ahead of them. "This ride takes ten people at a time. So it will be our turn next."

"**Blair** goes up, up!" **Harris** sang.

Martha patted **Harris's** back. "That's right, little buddy. **Blair** *and* **Harris** will go up, up and away on an **airplane**! **Very** soon now."

"Up, up, away," **Harris** repeated.

Harris

Chapter 2

Blair the **Bear** Takes Off

Harris stared at the balloon **carrying** his **bear** higher into the **air.** "Uh-oh. **Blair,** come back!"

Martha smoothed his **hair.** "Don't worry, **Harris.** Meg and Greg will get **Blair.** Let's go on the **airplane** ride while we wait."

• •

Greg ran with his eyes on the **bear.**

"Young man, look **where** you're going!" said a **parent carrying** a mountain of food.

"Sorry!" Greg called as he ran.

Meg stopped. "Please excuse us. We're trying to catch that teddy **bear!**"

The balloon floated toward a banner, and the **bear's** paw got caught.

air

Meg jumped off the **chair** and **carried** it back to the man's stall. Greg jogged after the balloon as it floated over the **fair**. Meg caught up with him near a **merry**-go-round.

"**Where** is **Blair**?" she asked.

"Over **there**." Greg pointed. "Floating toward the Super Slide."

Greg ran to the ticket collector. "Can we go up the **stairs** to catch that **bear**?"

The ticket collector pushed his **hair** out of his eyes. "Sure, kid. Good luck."

Chapter 3

A **Heron** Butts In

Greg raced toward the huge **Ferris** wheel. "The only way to get up **there** is to take the ride," he said, joining the line.

"Thank goodness this line is short," Meg said.

Greg nodded. "Martha must be wondering **where** we are."

Greg handed two tickets to the ticket collector.

"Enjoy your time on the **Ferris** Fun Ride!" she said.

Meg and Greg sat on a seat and waited.

The big wheel began to turn. Meg and Greg started moving up toward **Blair** the **bear**.

Meg and Greg were nearly at the top of the **Ferris** wheel when something flew past them.

Meg jumped. "Whoa! What was that?"

A large gray bird with a long beak landed on top of the sign next to **Blair.**

"That's a **heron**," Greg said.

"What's a **heron** doing at the fun **fair**?" Meg asked.

The **heron** pecked at the string holding the balloon on **Blair's** arm.

Greg flapped his hands. "Don't you **dare, heron**! Get away from our **bear.**"

Meg looked around for something to **scare** the bird away. All she could find was a few bits of popcorn.

Meg and Greg watched as the **heron** flew away with the **bear**.

"We nearly had him!" Meg said. "We nearly had **Blair** back."

Greg leaned out from his seat to keep his eyes on the **heron**. "We need to see **where** it takes **Blair**."

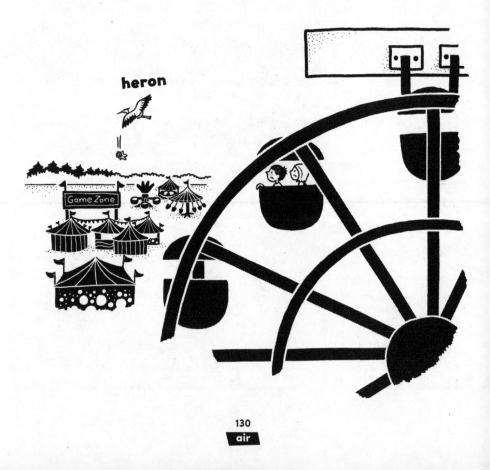

heron

Game Zone

air

Chapter 4

That's My **Bear**!

Thud!

"Mommy, Daddy, look! A teddy fell out of the sky!" cried a little girl. She yanked her hands from her **parents'** and ran toward **Blair**.

The girl's father looked up. "Good grief, **Nazair**! **Where** did that teddy **bear** fall from?"

Nazair bent down to pick up **Blair**. "Poor teddy **bear**. Are you OK?"

"I wonder who it belongs to," **Nazair's** mother said.

"Me! I will be the **bear's** mommy." **Nazair** squeezed **Blair** tightly.

"**Nazair**, honey, we can't just take the teddy **bear**. We have to find out who it belongs to."

Finally Meg and Greg could lift up the safety bar of the **Ferris** wheel and jump out of the seat.

"Come on, let's go!" Greg cried.

Together they dashed off toward the entrance to the Game Zone.

"**Where's** the fishing game?" Greg asked.

Meg pointed. "Over **there**. I see the sign."

"Hang on, **Blair**! We're coming!" Greg called as he and Meg ran through the crowds.

Meg and Greg explained **Blair's** adventure to **Nazair** and her **parents**.

"Well." **Nazair's** father chuckled. "That explains **where** the teddy fell from!"

Nazair's mother tried to gently pry **Blair** from the little girl's grip. "**Nazair**, honey. The teddy belongs to a little boy."

"I want to take **care** of the **bear**," **Nazair** sobbed. She kissed **Blair's** nose.

Greg crouched in front of **Nazair**. "Thank you for looking after the teddy for us."

"**Harris**, the little boy he belongs to, will be so happy that you found him!" Meg added.

fair

Win That **Bear**

Meg pointed at the row of game tents. "Let's play one of those games and try to win a teddy **bear** for her."

Greg nodded slowly. "We could try. I've never been **very** good at playing **fair** games."

"Me neither. But we can still try! Maybe we'll have good luck," Meg said.

"OK. Which one gives out teddy **bears** as prizes?" Greg asked.

Meg and Greg wandered along the row of tents.

Greg pulled a ticket out of his pocket and held it toward Meg. "Are you going to play?"

Meg nodded and stepped up to the tent. The attendant handed Meg three rings. "Here you go, kid. Throw them **carefully**!"

Meg tossed a ring at the row of glass bottles. *Clank!* The ring bounced off a bottle. She frowned and threw her next ring. *Clank!* She scowled and threw her last ring. *Clank!*

Meg blew the **hair** out of her eyes. "Three misses. That was **terrible**! You try, Greg."

Greg turned to Meg. "Could we give one of those prizes to **Nazair**?"

Meg shrugged. "Get an **airplane**, but let's try one more time for the **bear**."

She handed her last ticket to the attendant and nudged Greg. "You play. You did way better than I did."

Greg nodded, giving the toy **airplane** to Meg. "OK. This is our last chance to win a **bear** for little **Nazair**."

"You can do it, Greg," Meg said.

air

air

The End

Turn the page for more practice with the /air/ sound!

air sound
match-up

Draw a line from each word to the correct picture.

bear

pear

hair

chair

parrot

carrot

underwear

air sound
word search

Find the words listed below in the puzzle.
Words are hidden → and ↓.

```
p  f  a  r  c  y  b  a  v  o  m  f
a  l  r  a  r  k  x  i  o  l  a  u
r  a  m  r  t  h  e  r  e  f  r  n
e  r  c  e  c  o  x  c  h  l  e  f
n  e  h  s  t  a  i  r  b  a  g  a
t  k  a  z  s  w  e  a  r  i  l  i
a  r  i  d  r  g  s  f  z  r  c  r
h  e  r  o  n  r  i  t  a  h  j  c
```

airbag	flare	rare
aircraft	funfair	stair
arid	heron	swear
armchair	mare	there
flair	parent	

Also available at orcatworead.com

Some oddities of English explained

Do you know what's tricky about these words?

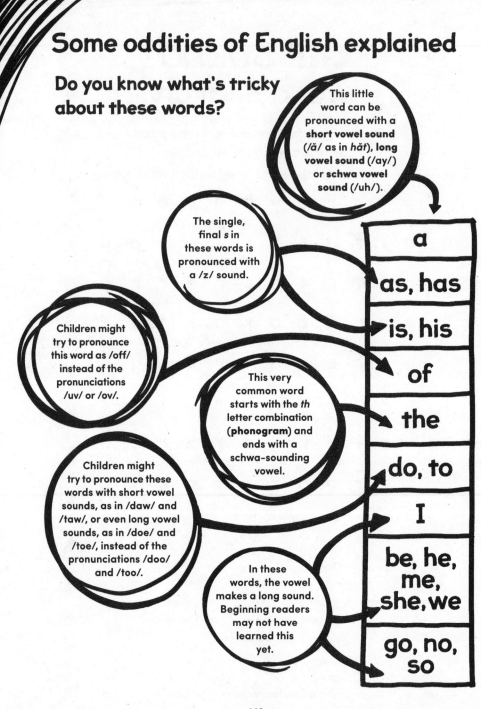

This little word can be pronounced with a **short vowel sound** (/ă/ as in *hăt*), **long vowel sound** (/ay/) or **schwa vowel sound** (/uh/).

The single, final *s* in these words is pronounced with a /z/ sound.

Children might try to pronounce this word as /off/ instead of the pronunciations /uv/ or /ov/.

This very common word starts with the *th* letter combination (**phonogram**) and ends with a schwa-sounding vowel.

Children might try to pronounce these words with short vowel sounds, as in /daw/ and /taw/, or even long vowel sounds, as in /doe/ and /toe/, instead of the pronunciations /doo/ and /too/.

In these words, the vowel makes a long sound. Beginning readers may not have learned this yet.

a

as, has

is, his

of

the

do, to

I

be, he, me, she, we

go, no, so

Children might try to pronounce this word as /ock/ instead of reading the two individual letters.

These words look like the **magic e** words, but they're not. The first vowel is pronounced with a short sound, and the final *e* is silent. Words in English never end with the letter *v*, so the final *e* is just there to protect the letter *v*.

This word is pronounced /y/-/oo/. It's fairly common for the letters *ou* to be pronounced with an /oo/ sound (*soup*), but beginning readers may not have learned this yet.

Words in the "all" family are pronounced /ŏ/-/l/. Beginning readers might try to pronounce the letter *a* as /ă/ as in *hăt*.

The *wh* **digraph** is pronounced as /w/ in most accents. All these question words are difficult to sound out (not only because of the *wh* but also because of the spelling of the rest of the word).

In this word, the letter *a* is pronounced with a short /ŭ/ sound, and the single, final *s* makes a /z/ sound.

OK

have, give

you

"all" family (ball, small, etc.)

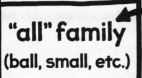

what, when, where, which, why

was

Why the multiple spellings for some of the sounds in this book's stories?

For the first time in the *Meg and Greg* series, we have written stories that introduce multiple spellings for a single sound. Most children who have worked their way through all the *Meg and Greg* stories in order, starting from Book 1: *A Duck in a Sock*, will have gained the reading skills and, we hope, the confidence to tackle reading these multiple spellings with support from a buddy reader. Parents and teachers may choose to teach the different spelling choices to children separately or all at once before reading the stories.

The multiple spellings are as follows:
- Story two, "A Lost Horse," the sound **/or/**: *or, oor* and *ore*
- Story three, "Surf Lessons," the sound **/er/**: *er, ir* and *ur*
- Story four, "The Bear in the Air," the sound **/air/**: *air, ear, ar*+vowel, *arr*+vowel, *er*+vowel and *err*+vowel

Are you sure it makes that sound?

Some of the **r-controlled vowels** are pronounced differently in different accents. This is especially the case for some of the **/air/** sounds, like in the words *heron* and *carrot*. We wrote these stories with Standard American English as our reference, so the first syllable in these words is pronounced /hair/ and /cair/. In some accents, however, these words will be pronounced a little differently. If this is the case for the child you're reading with, talk about these different pronunciations together, and perhaps make a list of these words and identify how they are pronounced in the child's accent.

A note about word endings

Known as suffixes, word endings are one or more letters added to the end of a word to change its function or meaning. In the first three *Meg and Greg* books, the only suffix we used was *-s* added to a base word, as in *cats*. We purposely avoided all other suffixes in the kid's text. However, when a child gets to this fourth book in the series, they are reading their thirteenth through sixteenth *Meg and Greg* stories. Wow!

By this stage in their reading progress, we think learning readers are ready to tackle more suffixes. For example, the suffix *-ing* (which includes the **phonogram** *ng* from Book 2) can be added to the base word *camp* to make *camping*. Sometimes the final letter of the base word gets doubled before the suffix attaches. For example, the suffix *-er* (which includes the phonogram *er* from story three of this book) can be added to the word *run* to make *runner*. Words that take suffixes in both of these ways (simple add-on and doubled final letter) are included in the Book 4 stories.

Some base words lose their final letter *e* before the suffix can be attached. For example, *bake* loses its *e* to take the suffix *-ing* and become *baking*. Words that lose their final letter *e* like this are not included in the Book 4 stories.

surfer dog

About the
Meg and Greg stories

Who are the Meg and Greg stories for?

These stories are for children who are struggling to learn how to read because they have **dyslexia** or another language-based learning difficulty.

We wrote the stories especially for struggling readers who are ages 6 to 9 (approximately grades 2–4), which is a little older than most kids start learning to read. These slightly older learners can understand and appreciate more complex content, but they need it written at a lower reading level. You might see this concept described with the term *hi-lo*.

To make a hi-lo concept work for children at a near-beginner reading level, we designed the *Meg and Greg* stories for shared reading. A buddy reader—an adult or other confident reader—shares the reading with the child who is learning. Each story has five short chapters and is ideal for use in one-on-one or small-group reading sessions.

Aren't there already lots of books for beginning readers?

Yes, but the many leveled readers available for beginners typically don't meet the needs of children with a learning difficulty. These children benefit from learning English incrementally and without spelling exceptions or advanced spellings thrown into the mix.

The *Meg and Greg* stories introduce one concept at a time. Each story builds on the previous ones by including words with the **phonograms**, spellings and sounds already introduced.

How does shared reading work?

Each story has several layers of text so that an adult or buddy reads the part of the story with more complex words and sentences, and the child reads the part of the story with carefully selected words and shorter sentences. Quite literally, *two read*.

Each story has:
- *Illustration labels* for a child just starting to read or feeling overwhelmed at reading sentences. The labels are single words or short phrases and contain the story's target letters as often as possible.

- *Kid's text* for a child who has mastered the basic **consonant** sounds (including **consonant blends**), **short vowel sounds** and the thirteen **phonograms** and spellings introduced in *Meg and Greg* Book 1 (*ck, sh, ch, th*), Book 2 (*nk, ng, tch, dge*) and Book 3 (*a-e, e-e, i-e, o-e, u-e*).

- *Kid's text* that always appears on the right-hand page when the book is open to a story. We also used kid's text for all story and chapter titles. As we created the stories, we bound ourselves to a set of rules that controlled the words we were "allowed" to use in the kid's text. If you're interested in these rules, they are listed on our website (orcatworead.com).

- *Adult or buddy reader's text*, which is the most difficult to read and always appears on the left-hand page when the book is open to a story. The buddy text uses longer sentences, a wider vocabulary and some letter combinations that the beginning reader has likely not yet learned, but it avoids very difficult words.

A child who is a more advanced reader and simply needs practice with the target concept can try reading all three layers of text in the story.

Are there any tips for buddy readers?

Yes! Try these ideas to help the child you're reading with:
- Keep the list of tricky words handy for the child to refer to when reading (see the lists on pages 148-149). Be patient! The child may need help each time they encounter a tricky word, even if they just read the word on the previous line of text.
- Before starting a story, have the child read the story title and each chapter title (in the table of contents). Ask them to predict what the story might be about.
- Before starting a story, make a list of all the words the child might not be familiar with and review them together.
- Before you read a page of buddy text, have the child point out all the words with the target concept on the left-hand page of the open book.
- After reading each chapter, have the child speak or write one sentence that uses some of the words from the chapter. Some children might like to draw a picture.

Do the stories use "dyslexia-friendly" features?

Yes. As well as the language features throughout the story, we used design features that some people find helpful for reading:
- The font mimics as closely as possible the shapes of hand-printed letters. Children begin by learning to print letters, so we think it is important for the letter shapes to be familiar. For example, a child learns to print *a* not a and *g* not g.
- The illustration labels are printed in lowercase letters as much as possible, because children often learn to recognize and write the lowercase alphabet first. A beginning reader may be less familiar with the uppercase letter shapes.
- The spaces between lines of text and between certain letters are larger than you might see in other books.
- The kid's text is printed on shaded paper to reduce the contrast between text and paper.

Glossary

/air/ sound: The sound introduced in the fourth story in this book. It is often spelled with the **phonogram** *air* as in *fair*. Less frequent spellings, also included in the fourth story, are *ear* (*bear*), *arr*+vowel (*parrot*), *ar*+vowel (*care*), *er*+vowel (*there*) and *err*+vowel (*Ferris*).

/ar/ sound: The sound introduced in the first story in this book. The sound is only spelled with the **phonogram** *ar* as in *farm*.

Consonant: Any letter in the alphabet except for the vowels (*a, e, i, o, u*).

Consonant blend: Two or three consonants appearing at the beginning or end of a syllable. Each consonant sound is pronounced, but the sounds are so close, they seem to be blended or "glued" together. For example, *flop, camp* and *sprint*.

Digraph: Two letters that together make one sound, such as *wh* in *what* and *th* in *thing*.

Dyslexia: A term made up of *dys*, meaning "difficult," and *lexis*, meaning "word." Dyslexia tends to be used as a catchall term for a range of language-learning difficulties. These can include reading (fluency and comprehension), spelling, writing, organization skills (executive function) and even some aspects of speech.

/er/ sound: The sound introduced in the third story in this book. The three most common **phonograms** for this sound are *er* (*her*), *ir* (*bird*) and *ur* (*turn*). Other ways to spell the sound /er/ (not included in this book) are the two suffixes *-or* as in *actor* and *-ar* as in *dollar* and also the phonograms *ar* (*orchard*), *ear* (*earth*), *our* (*journal*) and *yr* (*syrup*).

Long vowel sound: The way in English that a vowel sounds when we pronounce it for a long time (longer than for **short vowel sounds**) in regular speech. Long vowel sounds are often represented by a silent **magic e**, a combination of vowels or a single vowel occurring at the end of a syllable. For example, *bīke*, *mūte*, *rāin*, *trēe*, *gō*. The horizontal line, called a macron, shows that the vowel is pronounced with a long sound. Compare with short vowel sound.

Magic e: A silent (not pronounced) letter *e* at the end of a word to indicate that the previous vowel is pronounced with a long sound. Consider the difference between *măd* (**short vowel sound**) and *māde* (**long vowel sound**). Magic *e* words are the focus of *Meg and Greg* Book 3.

/or/ sound: The sound introduced in the second story in this book. It is most frequently spelled with the **phonogram** *or* as in *corn*. Two less frequent spellings, also included in the second story, are *oor* (*door*) and *ore* (*more*). Other ways to spell the sound /or/ (not included in this book) are *oar* (*board*), *our* (*four*) and *ar* when following a *w* (*war*, *warn*).

Phonogram: Any letter or combination of letters that represents one sound. For example, the sound /k/ can be spelled with five different phonograms: c (*cat*), k (*kite*), ck (*stick*), ch (*echo*) and que (*antique*).

r-controlled vowel(s): One or two vowels that are immediately followed by a letter r and whose pronunciation is controlled by that r. The pronunciation of the vowel(s) is very different from its short or long sound. Consider the difference between the pronunciation of the vowel in *băn* (**short vowel**) versus *barn* (r-controlled vowel) and in *hāil* (**long vowel**) versus *hair* (r-controlled vowel).

Schwa vowel sound: The way in English that we often pronounce the vowel in an unstressed syllable, like the *a* in *yoga*.

Short vowel sound: The way in English that a vowel sounds when we pronounce it for a short time in regular speech. For example, *ăt, nĕt, pĭg, tŏp* and *ŭp*.

Suffix: One or more letters added to the end of a word that change the word's function or meaning. Some common suffixes are -*s*, -*ing* and -*er*.

About the authors and illustrator

Who are the authors?

Elspeth and Rowena are sisters who believe in a world where all children learn to read with confidence and have the chance to discover the pleasure of being lost in a good book.

Elspeth is a teacher certified in using the Orton Gillingham approach to teach children with dyslexia and other language-based learning difficulties. She lives with her husband and three children in Vancouver, British Columbia.

Rowena is a children's writer and editor living with her two children in Victoria, British Columbia.

Elspeth

Rowena

Who is the illustrator?

Elisa

Elisa is an award-winning children's book designer, illustrator and author with a passion for language and literacy. Originally from Mexico City, she lives with her husband and two children in Vancouver, British Columbia.

Acknowledgments

We have many people to thank for helping us create this fourth book in the *Meg and Greg* series. Huge thanks to our editors, Liz Kemp, Ruth Linka and Vanessa McCumber, at Orca Book Publishers for their unwavering support and guidance. We're also very grateful to Orca's amazing editing, design and marketing teams, and to Susan Korman, who reviewed the stories and gave us invaluable feedback.

We asked several families and students to test-read the stories and activities, and we thank them all for their comments and encouragement. They are Rosetta de Jong, Edie and Hazel Kemp, Maleah and Kimberley McKenzie, Hazel and Elliot McNally, Kimberley Wahl and Eliot and Madeleine Wilson. We also thank several of Elspeth's students at Blundell Elementary in the Richmond School District, and in particular Vivian Lam's class.

We wrote these stories while staying on Pender Island, which is one of our favorite BC Gulf Islands. We give Pender a special thanks for all the inspiration!

Elisa gives special thanks to Dave, Daniel and Jay for their patience and support during the long hours of work on the series.

Thank you, readers, for joining Meg and Greg on their adventures on Stardust Island. We hope you found the stories as fun to read as we did to write and illustrate!